D0850526

MIND AND MAN

MIND AND MAN

THE KINGDOM OF HEAVEN
A PRESENT REALITY

MARTHA WILCOX

*"Though Empires Fall,
the Lord shall reign forever."*

The Bookmark
Santa Clarita, California

Wilcox, Martha.
  Mind and man : the kingdom of heaven a present
reality / by Martha Wilcox.
    p. cm.
    LCCN 2005928145
    ISBN-13: 978-0-930227-79-1
    ISBN-10: 0-930227-79-4

  1. Christian Science. 2. Consciousness—Religious
aspects—Christianity.   I. Title.

  BX6945.W635 2005   289.5
                                QBI05-600073

Published by
The Bookmark
Post Office Box 801143
Santa Clarita, California 91380

MORTALS may have a big belief of brain, but according to Christian Science the claim that somebody thinks blinds man to the fact that there is but one Mind, God, and consequently only one real *thinker* and one *thought*. "The Lord of hosts hath sworn, saying, Surely as I have thought so shall it come to pass; and as I have purposed, so shall it stand." (Isaiah 14:24)

When man begins to see himself as the reflection of God, Mind, and recognizes all power from Him in whom we live and move and have our being, he has reached the highest of all endowments and fruitful of all good works. *He who is obedient to Truth has immense power for service.* The truth frees him from ignorance of his capacities and privileges. It fortifies and sustains him under all circumstances. It is here and now. Pentecostal power is always present. It is the power of Mind enabling man to do the will of wisdom, for God's biddings are always enablings. It is the power to think, to act, to speak, so that life is fruitful and joyous. It is the capacity every man possesses to act in harmony with divine power, and this is to preserve a scientific sense of being.

Nothing is truth but the absolute. We do not know anything. Mind is the only source of power. Thought is the only force. Therefore, those who have turned to the fountainhead of Being for the solution of any problem, have brought such titanic force into intelligent activity that the results may seem incredible. Principle does not require time to become itself and find true expression. Mind is causative. We reflect the ideas of Mind, interpret them to ourselves and objectify or bring out the fruit of thought. Therefore, the word of God spoken into consciousness is the seed bearing fruit after its kind.

MARY BAKER EDDY

MIND AND MAN
THE KINGDOM OF HEAVEN A PRESENT REALITY

"Though empires fall, the Lord shall reign forever."

Martha Wilcox

When Mary Baker Eddy revealed Mind as God, therefore one, she revealed that the act of creating is an act or function of Mind. Since Mind is the Mind of all men, creation as thought is the individual experience of each one, and the act of creating as the function of Mind is the individual experience of each one. The mind of Mind's manifestation, man, would necessarily have to be Mind. A true thinker is one who thinks from this standpoint of the one Mind. This correct thinking naturally brings about the disappearance of the belief that mind is human or mortal. Such thinkers do not think the truth about creation, but they think the Truth itself, and this is creation or revelation — Mind's self-revealingness. This is the creation which is ever appearing fresh, new, original.

Human sense, which is ignorant of God, *misinterprets* the substance and tangibility of this revelation which is creation, and calls it matter. This ignorance of God is entirely supposition; and so any change which seems to take place in our world is simply in the appearance of things, since there could be no change in the reality; and what appears as change is a thinning of the mist of ignorance and a clearer vision of Truth — error disappearing and Truth, to that extent, appearing.

1

It is the province of the Christian Scientist to decide what the activity is which apparently confronts him. In Science all that is, is something Mind is comprehending and expressing as itself. What he decides is true, what he feels, sees, and hears, is true to him. He is not influenced by personal deceit or strivings, but acknowledges that the activity he beholds and experiences is the operation of Principle unfolding as the changeless good. This scientific recognition reveals his present experience — his universe, which is the infinity of his body — as under the control of Principle and thus unvarying in its harmony, regardless of how material it may appear to human sense. Mrs. Eddy states in *Science and Health with Key to the Scriptures*, "Mind is the master of the corporeal senses, and can conquer sickness, sin and death. Exercise this God-given authority. Take possession of your body and govern its feeling and action," and in *Miscellaneous Writings* she adds, "The full understanding that God is Mind, and that matter is but a belief, enables you to control pain."

One's present experience is entirely a question of viewpoint or standpoint from which one is thinking, and this is shown in *Science and Health*: "This testimony of Holy Writ sustains the fact in Science, that the heavens and earth to one human consciousness, that consciousness which God bestows, are spiritual, while to another, the unillumined human mind, the vision is material. This shows unmistakably that what the human mind terms matter and spirit indicates states and stages of consciousness."

The Christian Scientist, understanding that all consciousness is Mind and Mind is God, has no temptation to identify what appears as his universe with matter. He understands that spiritual consciousness, conceiving everything after its own nature, Spirit, conceives everything that he could possibly be aware of, after that perfect indestructible nature. Thus he separates himself from the false picture which is claiming to be part of his consciousness.

2

The Christian Scientist does not go about saying, "I am not material," but he refuses to entertain the material sense, which is all there is to what is called his materiality. In *Unity of Good* Mrs. Eddy tells us, ". . . this spiritual consciousness can form nothing unlike itself, Spirit, and Spirit is the only creator." The only Mind there is, knows now and forever the oneness of itself. Anyone accepting this fact of the one Mind can demonstrate and prove for himself the end of error.

True consciousness is not something to be gained. It is already the Mind of man. Even when something seems to go wrong and is claiming to dull one's realization, all there is, is the divine idea, which so-called human sense interprets materially; therefore, we cannot outline the divine idea and say it is this or that, but we can decide that since all that is called matter is Mind, nothing has existed but the idea of God which assumes different forms as the human belief disappears.

All that you apparently behold is within that which you accept as consciousness. What is consciousness to you? In *Unity of Good* Mrs. Eddy states, "All consciousness is Mind; and Mind is God, — an infinite, and not a finite consciousness. This consciousness is reflected in individual consciousness, or man, whose source is infinite Mind. There is no really finite mind, no finite consciousness. There is no material substance, for Spirit is all that endureth, and hence is the only substance. There is, can be, no evil mind, because Mind is God. God and His ideas — that is, God and the universe — constitute all that exists. Man, as God's offspring, must be spiritual, perfect, eternal." And again in *Science and Health* she adds, "To understand that Mind is infinite, not bounded by corporeality, not dependent upon the ear and eye for sound or sight, nor upon muscles and bones for locomotion, is a step towards the Mind-science by which we discern man's nature and existence . . . This Soul-sense comes to the human mind when the latter yields to the divine Mind."

Right practice requires that we deal with our entire experience as a mental experience. The impersonal Word of God, (unfoldment), is what appears to sense as persons and things — the language with which God describes Himself.

Religion

A religious system that creates a future good is abstract, because its good is postponed. All the good which will ever be, Science reveals, is the good which we are now. Christian Science is the one practical religion, since it teaches that Life lives as us; that Mind, ever aware of its own infinitude, is the awareness which we are. The practice of this religion means that we be what we are by letting right ideas constitute the whole of our consciousness and understanding — that is, those ideas that are ourselves and our universe.

Heaven is not a future experience, but it is the orderly unfoldment of the one divine Being, which is the "I" of each one of us. Religion is really an acknowledgment of our identification with God and is entirely a *within* experience, never *without*. Religion is living Life as it really is, and means living Life within, not from without.

Our Church is a structure of Truth and Love, and this Church can give proof of its utility and elevate the race only when Truth and Love are demonstrated as the consciousness of the individual. Religion becomes of the head and not of the heart, if we believe that Truth becomes real simply because someone else is thinking it; our own understanding and consciousness of God is not something which can be inherited or derived from another.

4

Luke records Christ Jesus' remarks on this: "And when he was demanded of the Pharisees, when the kingdom of God should come, he answered them and said, The kingdom of God cometh not with observation: Neither shall they say, Lo here! or, lo there! for, behold, the kingdom of God is within you.

Human vs. Spiritual Concept

We must understand that what is called a human concept, is a viewpoint, an interpretation, the way the divine idea appears to human sense. A viewpoint is not a created something with entity or identity to be resisted or resented or loved or cherished. In reality there is no human concept since there is no mind to perceive imperfectly or entertain a finite sense of the infinite.

The so-called mind which gives identity to the human concept as something, is a suppositional mind which our textbook calls *mortal mind*. Mrs. Eddy defined this term as a solecism, since Mind is immortal, and which she said could be used in teaching Christian Science to designate that which is unreal. It is not necessary then, from the standpoint of the practice of Christian Science, to take up arms against it, since it is wholly suppositional mind. This suppositional mind includes within itself all there is to a sick, sinning, dying mortal.

Materially, therefore, we cannot outline the divine idea and say it is this or that; but we can decide that since all that is called matter is Mind, *nothing has existence but the idea of God which assumes different forms as the human belief disappears*. In the textbook, *Science and Health*, our Leader writes, "Creation is ever appearing, and must ever continue to appear from the nature of its inexhaustible source. Mortal sense inverts this appearing and calls ideas material. Thus misinterpreted, the divine idea seems to fall to the level of a human or material belief, called mortal man." In *Miscellaneous Writings* she says, ". . . every creation or idea of Spirit has its counterfeit in some matter belief. Every material belief hints the existence of spiritual reality."

This has been generally accepted as if there were a material belief actually existing, whereas a human concept is a figure of speech, or a word describing a spiritual event to those who can look beyond their present senses.

Since conception means comprehension, or perception, what is called the human concept is some perception, or comprehension, or understanding of Truth, and is actually the divine idea appearing according to the clarity of our vision or the lessening of the belief. There is no human concept; there is no roar of the lion; it is the inaudible voice of Truth. It is ignorance, finite sense, which claims to limit what the spiritual sense beholds, the true idea, which is everything that exists in Mind as Mind. Therefore, *the spiritual consciousness which you are, finds everything in Mind as its manifestation*. We read in the textbook, "The divine Mind, not matter, creates all identities, and they are forms of Mind, the ideas of Spirit apparent only as Mind, never as mindless matter nor the so-called material senses." Since there is no human mind to conceive of God, the human concept is a concept mind to conceive of God; the human mind concept is an inference drawn from a fact. One's ability to have any conception of God is because the Mind of man is God.

Counterfeit, as used in Christian Science, does not mean a created something copying the real, but it does mean that imperfect apprehension, ignorance and false belief creates to human sense an illusion like a mirage, a ghost. Since all is infinite Mind and its infinite manifestation, nothing exists but the manifestation with all the characteristics of Mind. "There are not two, — Mind *and* matter. We must get rid of that notion. As we commonly think, we imagine all is well if we cast something into the scale of Mind, but we must realize that Mind is not put into the scales with matter; then only are we working on one side and in Science," Mrs. Eddy writes in *Miscellaneous Writings*.

The Christian Scientist thinks of the universe, his body, his friends, in terms of what he understands God to be. It is his understanding that determines his viewpoint; it is the correct view which makes a change in the appearance of his world. He does not make a graven image of anything in the heaven above or the earth beneath to bow down to or serve by letting it make him unhappy or happy.

As idea or reflection, man is the conscious identity of being, and therefore is the embodiment of all that is true about God. All that you are experiencing at any time, you are experiencing as the one divine embodiment — Mind as its infinite manifestation. In this understanding, all is harmony and boundless bliss. "In different ages the divine idea assumes different forms, according to humanity's needs." (ibid)

Mary, or woman, as our textbook states, perceived the spiritual idea, and called her conception Jesus. There was no thought of Jesus, either in what is called Mary's consciousness, or in the consciousness of those who prophesied the Saviour; but Mind, ever unfolding and redeeming consciousness from the belief of finiteness, revealed an idea of man's Christ that they called Jesus. The Christ, the divine manifestation of God, was never Jesus, the highest human corporeal concept; but Jesus, the concept, was the Christ unfolding as individual consciousness, and they called this idea of the oneness of being which they discerned, Jesus. The servant of Elisha perceived an idea of God and called his conception horses and chariots of fire. John, the beloved

Revelator, perceived an idea of God and called his conception Bride, a city foursquare, the tree of Life whose leaves were for the healing of the nations.

When Paul perceived an idea of God, his conception was a light so bright that it blinded him, he lost his material sense of sight. Idea is not outlined by persons, but through Science we perceive an idea of God, and this idea is a conception of God appearing in a form apprehensible to us.

Since all form, outline, color, substance are in Mind, our figures of speech appear to possess all of these elements. There is no beauty, no outline, no form in the figure of speech. When we actually understand that all that is going on is Mind infinitely manifesting itself in the perception of its idea, and that this manifestation or selfhood of Mind is the being which is ourselves, any suggestion that things are material or that we lack any good thing will make no impression on us.

From this standpoint we can declare that what we are seeing and hearing is good. From this standpoint there would be no temptation to look to the human concept and expect it to change or be healed, since you would expect the finite concept to disappear. We are the divine creation in the measure that we rise above the belief or sense that creation is material. When thought is entirely free from any sense of persons and things, what we see is the idea and not a human concept. We see the invisible things of Him being seen when understood.

When we accept the false belief that there is a divine idea back of a material concept, one must accept the belief of two minds; but when one understands the revelation of Science, that Mind is one, the so-called material symbol is to that consciousness the divine idea appearing. The beauty, form, outline and color, so dimly perceived, is the beauty, form, outline and color of the divine Mind. Mrs. Eddy tells us this in *Science and Health*, "Beauty is a thing of life, which dwells forever in the eternal Mind and reflects the charms of His goodness in expression, form, outline, and color. It is Love which paints the petal with myriad hues, glances in the warm sunbeam, arches the cloud with the bow of beauty, blazons the night with starry gems, and covers earth with loveliness."

Your identity and dominion consists in your ability to discern the divine idea and disregard the limited concept which claims to dull your vision. It is a serious mistake to think that the concept possesses good and useful qualities, no matter how good and useful it may seem to be. A Christian Scientist appreciates and enjoys the concept, however it may look to human sense, because to him it is the divine idea — Mind's representation of itself — appearing. That which divides the divine idea and the human concept, making two, is viewpoint. The belief that an understanding of God is not God's understanding of Himself, but is man's, results in what seems to be degrees of understanding, as the concept which appears is determined by the clarity of our vision. If the human concept were not simply viewpoint or the way the divine idea appears, those things which are valuable, useful, and in fact absolutely necessary to our present sense of living, could not even seem to be. Of what value would be the figure "2" divorced from the mathematical idea? Its whole being is as the mathematical idea. Since its existence is as the mathematical idea, it is always available to you and me at the same time.

If it disappears, it can be recalled for our use. Would the mathematical idea be of any value to us without the figure "2" and would the figure "2" be of any value divorced from the idea? The idea might just as well not exist if it did not appear to our present sense of seeing. Truth is not abstract. An idea of God seems abstract to human sense and far removed from what apparently is appearing as our universe; but abstract Truth is concrete being since an idea, being the understanding of what actually is, is tangible and visible. What finite sense interprets as matter is actually some conception of Truth. "I believe that of which I am conscious through the understanding, however faintly able to demonstrate Truth and Love," Mrs. Eddy writes in *Unity of Good*, and more specifically in *Science and Health*, "Mortal mind sees what it believes as certainly as it believes what it sees. It feels, hears, and sees its own thoughts. Pictures are mentally formed before the artist can convey them to canvas. So is it with all material conceptions."

A Christian Scientist accepts as real only what he is conscious of through his understanding. He sees what he believes, but never believes what he sees. The important question is, what is a chair, a mountain to you? That which calls a thing material constitutes the only materiality it has. "Material sense defines all things materially, and has a finite sense of the infinite." "Science declares that Mind, not matter, sees, hears, feels, speaks. Whatever contradicts this statement is the false sense, which ever betrays mortals into sickness, sin, and death." (ibid)

Whatever we see through eyes, hear through ears, etc. is actually idea, since Mind alone is consciousness or awareness. It is in that consciousness alone that we see what we think we see with our eyes, hear with our ears, feel with our fingers. Since consciousness is Mind and Mind is God, let us look into Mind and find the facts of being which finite sense misinterprets, reverses, and calls material things. The world we think we see, exists in the consciousness of each individual and actually is a product, as well as the presence, of the Mind which is God. "The periods of spiritual ascension are the days and seasons of

Mind's creation, in which beauty, sublimity, purity, and holiness — yea, the divine nature — appear in man and the universe never to disappear." (ibid)

When one considers anything from the standpoint of the human concept, what it is, how it is, where it is, one denies God as the only consciousness, and to attribute power to any cause but God is to declare our own powerlessness.

We are confronted with seeming changes in our universe, some of them very revolutionary. The more revolutionary the seeming changes the better, since they indicate the passing away of false concepts and the evolution of the spiritual idea. The divine idea appears according to divine law, and the concepts disappear and reappear according to that law. We must not outline how this will seem to human sense, since any attempt to outline God, ascribes to God the limitations of the human mind. The divine idea actually never changes, never disappears and reappears, since God is omnipresence and His idea is likewise ever present. The discernment of this ever presence which is ever appearing in greater effulgence is misinterpreted as the disappearing and reappearing of what we call human concepts.

Substance

When the things that to human sense seem valuable and useful disappear, and do not seem to reappear in a fairer form, we may be certain that we have accepted the belief that they exist as matter and not as an idea. The human concept which seems to be in matter is a mental picture trying to make us believe that substance can be destroyed. "We should learn whether they govern the body through a belief in the necessity of sickness and death, sin and pardon, or govern it from the higher understanding

11

that the divine Mind makes perfect, acts upon the so-called human mind through truth, leads the human mind to relinquish all error, to find the divine Mind to be the only Mind, and the healer of sin, disease, death. This process of higher spiritual understanding improves mankind until error disappears, and nothing is left which deserves to perish or to be punished." (ibid)

Note the marginal note: "Mortal mind's disappearance." Therefore this false belief that things exist as human concepts or as matter, hides the ever present idea. "Every object in material thought will be destroyed," since there is no mortal mind, and so long as we think of things as matter, there will be lack. "If Mind is within and without all things, then all is Mind; and this definition is scientific." (ibid)

This present lack will continue in some form until handled through Science. We are shown how to do this in *Miscellaneous Writings*: "Christ Jesus' sense of matter was the opposite of that which mortals entertain — His earthly mission was to translate substance into its original meaning, Mind."

No matter how beautiful the human concept, how good it seems to be, how useful, that does not save it from disappearing; but if the disappearance of the concept is understood to be a clearer vision of the divine idea unfolding as individual consciousness, then the disappearing and the reappearing of concepts will not be in the nature of painful revolution or chemicalization. Nor will there seem to be interruption of the continuity of good, but as beauty, order, joy, harmony forever unfolding in clearer measure as ourselves and our universe. Ignorance of God is all there is to matter, and this ignorance constitutes a suppositional realm operating without a cause.

I am often asked why a person who has no spiritual understanding may seem to possess unlimited wealth and health. In reality, since all things that the Father hath the son hath, abundance of good is the possession of each one. Unless that person is recognizing that every gift is of God, the belief that possessions are material will so dull his perception of Truth that eventually those possessions will seem to disappear. Mrs. Eddy once said, "If we do not control our possessions through the understanding that they are spiritual, they will control us through the belief that they are material."

That which endures and satisfies springs from Truth, and is never separated from the justification of itself which is Principle. Are we thinking from the standpoint of Principle and thus entertaining the correct view? Then there will be the appearing more and more of the divine reality, and the disappearing of that which calls itself a human concept. The wholeness of the Divine Being is appearing now as the individuality of each one of us; and nothing is lost by giving up the false concept; in fact, the willingness to give up the limited view is the first step in a clearer vision of reality.

Mrs. Eddy tells us in the textbook, ". . . the human self must be evangelized. This task God demands us to accept lovingly to-day, and to abandon so fast as practical the material, and to work out the spiritual which determines the outward and actual." When she speaks about the evangelizing of the human self, she does not mean that there is any human being to be changed or evangelized in the old sense, but that the human belief must be given up for the divine idea, which man actually is.

Reformation is giving up the false sense of self. This process of giving up appears to human sense as a human being learning about God; but actually the ideas which seem to come to that human being are the disappearance of the human and the appearance of the divine. Do not think of yourself as a person striving to know about God, since that is not true; you *are* idea, reflection, the divine Mind reflecting itself as all-inclusive, harmonious, perfect consciousness. Your experience is the understanding of God, which is the reality of all things brought to light; there should be no attempt to make the human being Godlike. Evangelization is a clearer vision of God, and this idea of God, which is your true selfhood appearing, operates in our present sense of right as a better human.

It is only when we interpret things materially that we have trouble. Hell is materialism consuming itself, material and personal beliefs proving themselves nothing; and our world will be a hell to us so long as we associate or identify ourselves with matter or personal sense, since there is no matter or personality; and this spiritual fact must be continually appearing; hence the seeming destruction and disintegration observable when anything is "outside" as matter or personality.

Personality

What is called matter or personality is material belief or material sense, and must be constantly fulfilling the conditions of its nothingness. We are not dealing with a substance called matter or a personality, but merely with a belief that misrepresents substance or man. Matter appears to disintegrate and decay since it is a belief that being is finite and that power is destruction. When it is understood that man is an idea of God and not a human person, and this understanding heals him of what seems to be a physical disease, this proves that his body is not material. It is only the belief in evil or matter that bears the fruits of matter or self destruction. The textbook tells us, "A mortal belief fulfils its own conditions. Sickness, sin, and death are the vague realities of human conclusions. Life, Truth, and Love are the realities of divine Science. They dawn in faith and glow full-orbed in spiritual understanding. As a cloud hides the sun it cannot extinguish, so false belief silences for a while the voice of immutable harmony, but false belief cannot destroy Science armed with faith, hope, and fruition." (ibid)

Therefore we can rejoice when what seems to be a manifestation of evil is understood as the uncovering and consequent disappearance of a false belief of error, revealing the nothingness of matter, and the permanency and indestructibility of Spirit. Joy is an idea and is apprehensible, appearing to our present sense of sight as conditions and systems through which we seem to derive joy. In other words, all that is really happening where so much evil is apparent, is a clearer vision of Principle. Until it is seen that personal or material sense is all there is to what is called matter, matter will seem to be destroyed, or to fulfill the conditions of its own unreality through what is humanly called disease and death. This process does not destroy matter since what is called matter is not something that can be destroyed. What is called matter, being a misstatement of Mind, can only disappear through translation — spiritual education — and this is really a disappearance of nothing, and the revealing of things as they are — a finite sense of the infinite. Matter is simply imperfect apprehension. In *Miscellaneous Writings* Mrs. Eddy states it this way: "For matter to be matter, it must have been self-created. Mind has no more power to evolve or to create matter than has good to produce evil. Matter is a misstatement of Mind; it is a lie, claiming to talk and disclaim against Truth; idolatry, having other gods; evil, having presence and power over omnipotence!"

Science does not teach that we lift ourselves out of material existence into spiritual existence. There is only one existence, and through Christian Science we lose a material sense of spiritual existence. Christian Science is an interpretation of existence as it really is, identifying all that we are conscious of as an idea of Mind, while the claim is that there is a material body or a human concept to be disposed of. The attempt to dispose of the human as if it were something, is the warfare between Spirit and the flesh. The student of Christian Science who shuns the human concept of what seems to be a material object because he thinks it is matter, and attempts to dispose of it like the ascetic, by striving to hold himself physically and mentally aloof, misinterprets Science and robs himself of good.

We do not attempt to destroy erroneous mental images. When we understand their nature as illusion this proves them nothing. We must understand the meaning of the term error or evil and matter, and this understanding is the specific handling of the claim that they exist as something to cope with. To understand that "evil and all its forms are inverted good" would certainly meet the belief that evil was something to be destroyed. To understand matter as substance, a perishable sense of the imperishable, would meet the belief that matter is substance. Since there is no matter, the belief of life and substance as matter includes in its deceptive sense its self-destruction, and this false sense appears objectively as fear and disease. So to state, "There is no disease," or, "There is no fear," does not take care of the difficulty since it is not a belief of disease, but a belief of matter as substance.

Judaism

Someone asks "What are we to do with the so-called Jewish problem." Christian Science gives us the solution. Since Christian Science is the Christ, the Christ, or the true knowledge of God and man, is the answer to the Jewish problem.

Judaism is not a race of people, but a viewpoint. Even Paul said that Christ cannot be divided into Jew and Gentile, bond or free. When we understand that Judaism is a type of thinking, then we will see that the Jew is not persecuted by any group or nation. The false belief of being a Jew with all that it implies, includes the persecution of that belief, and this appears as persecution and persecutors. Actually what seems to be persecution is self-righteousness and the love of materiality, destroying itself. Just as in the case of Cain and Able, as Mrs. Eddy says in the textbook, "The erroneous belief that life, substance and intelligence can be material ruptures the life and brotherhood of man at the very outset." Judaism is the anti-Christ, that which divides humanity into the chosen and the unchosen — those who keep the law and those who do not. The Christ cannot be divided.

Revolution

Let us understand that revolution is always the birth of a new order and not the destruction of anything, and *it is imposed by the pressure of Truth*. Human intelligence must be uncovered as nothing before it can disappear. Until human intelligence is seen to be a deception, anything resulting from its cultivation is dangerous and destructive, because it is material. Thought must be divested of its belief in matter or personality before the spiritual facts of being can appear. It is the pure in heart that see God. So long as the convenience and enjoyment of everyday living are associated with human intelligence, or with personal effort for accomplishment, joy has no permanence and hope is a cheat. In fact, the very thing which seems such a blessing, and would be if correctly identified, can because of false identification appear afflictive and destructive.

17

When those conveniences which liberate humanity from the limitations incidental to a belief of a material existence, are understood as Mind unfolding as individual consciousness, it will be seen that the divine idea can never assume forms that burden or harm, but are always contributive and blessing. The attainments of the human race are not due to the human intelligence of personal striving, but to the fact that God is Mind, and therefore these attainments or inventions would never appear destructive if understood as Mind, and not as matter. Mind cannot manifest itself as anything destructive or afflictive. Mind's manifestation or idea must appear in a form which meets humanity's need. If we through ignorance make unto ourselves a graven image, identify ourselves with an automobile that can injure or a gun that can kill, we must unmake such an image, since no such thing can possibly exist.

It is only as one reasons from the standpoint that all existence is consciousness and consciousness is Mind, God, that one can proceed in the scientific path of demonstrating a universe with no inventions that are afflictive and destructive, and a universe which appears to you fairer each day because error disappears as painlessly as two times two equals five.

If we think of God separate from ourselves, God is not understood, and therefore is unknown to us. This is Mind's universe; everything exists as a divine idea, God's idea of Himself; and this idea is His reflection man, embracing all the actualities of infinite expression. The reflection of God (what God knows Himself to be) is as necessary to God as God is to the reflection, since without reflection God could not exist. We need never be afraid that God will be man or man will be God. That which is essential to each other cannot be each other or be interchangeable with each other. That which is source or cause cannot take the place of the effect, nor can effect take the place of cause; and yet cause is not cause without that of which it is the cause, and effect is not effect without that of which it is the effect.

Reflection

The dictionary tells us that "to reflect is to think," and since Mind is the only thinking agent, Mind, God, does all of the reflecting. Through Science you perceive the facts of God. That perception is you, but it is also God, since only Mind perceives what God is; therefore, man as reflection is Mind saying, "I AM THAT I AM." Reflection is the mode of operation or faculty by which Mind has knowledge of itself and its operations. When you use the word *reflection* be sure that you do not think of it as something outside of its source, or outside of Mind. God, as the one source or cause, constitutes His creation, which is His own self-consciousness or reflection. Scientific reflection, therefore, is included in its source. Mind, reflecting itself to itself, is the reflection we call man.

In Christian Science we do not deal with things objectively perceived, but with ideas, subjective reflection, which means that all that apparently confronts us must be seen as something we are experiencing within our own mind. For us to interpret what we seem to see as something going on outside of the divine consciousness, Mind, would be an attempt to objectify reflection. Something that you seem to behold, is part of the divine consciousness which you are. If we were not equipped with the power of thought, we would experience nothing. Let us understand that it is the intelligence and activity of our own divine Mind, God, that we are beholding, however it may appear to finite sense. Since Mind is one, whatever we seem to behold humanly, being some concept of what is divinely going on, is actually a divine experience in Mind, and therefore included in the divine reflection called man. This divine reflection, man, cannot be included in anything, for God is all inclusive. Therefore, His reflection is all inclusive. Man is the all inclusive consciousness which includes everything as idea. The two words *manifestation* and *reflection* do not exactly mean the same, and yet when one understands that God is All, the terms can be used interchangeably.

Manifestation refers to God in His relation to man. "All is infinite Mind and its infinite manifestation, for God is All-in-all," *Science and Health* records. Man, to exist must have a cause, and that cause is God self-manifested and self-revealing; so the term *manifestation* indicates the essentialness of God to man and the universe. Reflection refers to man in his relation to God. Mind would be a non-entity without an awareness or idea of itself. In other words, God would not know what He is in all the infinity of His being, without reflecting or turning back on Himself, and this reflection is man. So the term reflection indicates the essentialness of man to God, the importance of man as the knowledge or understanding whereby God, the first great cause, is known. The terms God and man are equally important.

God without a knowledge of Himself would be without an idea, and therefore would be no God. The son can do nothing of himself, but what he reflects or knows of the Father, for whatsoever the Father, Mind, reflects or knows Himself to be, there also the son likewise knows himself to be.

It is the correct understanding of reflection as God's knowledge of His own infinite nature, that is important for us in our understanding of ourselves. There is no justification for man except as God's reflection of Himself. Until we understand man as reflection, as the understanding of God, which understanding is the true I, or Christ, the false concept of man will seem to separate us from God, and thus we seem bereft of our God-bestowed power and dominion.

Man

Man is simply a term to express Mind as manifestation. Therefore, it is not man you are conscious of, but God as infinite manifestation. When you use the word God it means Mind and its infinite manifestation. "The Principle of all cure is God, unerring and immortal Mind." We find this in *Miscellaneous Writings*.

The reflection of God which is man, must be God reflecting Himself to Himself. It would be a denial of God as All, to think of man as having any entity or identity of his own. God and man are like a single word, which when broken apart makes no sense — God in man. When you perceive and declare God is Love, this is an idea of God. Mind is knowing itself to be Love. This idea which your Mind, God, entertains of itself is you. To express it another way, since you are an idea of God, the understanding of God which you have constitutes the idea which you are. This divine knowledge which emanates from Mind and manifests Mind, is as harmonious, intelligent and joyful as its source, since all that constitutes this idea or understanding is Truth, which is Mind itself. Man is in the restful position of having nothing to do, nothing to achieve, nothing to accomplish, since as reflection he is changeless, joyous, all-inclusive being, forever at peace. Man is simply a term to express God's awareness of Himself as all; therefore, it is not man that your mind reflects, but it is Mind as its own infinite manifestation.

Almighty is a translation of the Hebrew word *Shaddai*, meaning the breasted one, the nourisher one, or sustainer, the all-sufficient one, Principle. So *El Shaddai* not only expresses God as cause or creator, but expresses His relationship to all that He has created — His power to maintain creation. Creator is not something that begins something, but that which keeps the universe going. The term God is not in itself sufficient to express the real meaning of God, since God is not God without that which God is God to. When you use the word God you must understand that it means omnipotent, omnipresent, omniscient Being, which is Principle as cause and idea as effect. "Principle and its idea is one and this one is God," "All is infinite Mind and its infinite manifestation." These statements are from *Science and Health*.

Unless you can use the word God consciously aware that it means Principle and its idea, do not use it; use the synonyms as given in the textbook. In expressing the oneness of Being, Mind is a particularly good synonym to use, since there is no temptation to believe that man and his Mind can be separated.

Compound means a combination of elements which make one. This compound being, Principle, called God, is reflected as the compound idea called man. This man reflects the creative Principle which reproduces the multitudinous forms of Mind. In *Science and Health* we read, "The universe of Spirit reflects the creative power of the divine Principle, or Life, which reproduces the multitudinous forms of Mind and governs the multiplication of the compound idea man."

When you consider this one divine Being, God, you must understand that it is Principle and idea. When you consider this one divine Being as man, you must understand that it is the embodiment of the full nature of God, or as *No and Yes* states, "One Mind, a perfect man, and divine Science." The divine Mind can make no discrimination between itself and the reflection of itself. "True idealism is a divine Science, which combines in logical sequence, nature, reason, and revelation. An effect without a cause is inconceivable; neither philosophy nor reason attempts to find one; but all should conceive and understand that Spirit cannot become less than Spirit; hence that the universe of God is spiritual, — even the ideal world whose cause is the self-created Principle, with which its ideal or phenomenon must correspond in quality and quantity." This is from *Miscellaneous Writings*.

The fact that God is All-in-all does not make man a nonentity, but gives him individuality and identity, since his existence is necessary to God, and Soul is his body or identity. This man is Life living itself; his Mind, minding itself. "Christ presents the indestructible man, whom Spirit creates, constitutes, and governs," the textbook states. And Soul is his body or identity. He is unassailed and unassailable since nature and essence is Truth. He is not truthful; he is Truth itself reflected and expressed. The reason or law of his being is Principle; therefore, there is no variation in its continuity. He is Love, forever being Love; therefore, man is reflection or image and must be Love. One might make a mistake in an endeavor to be loving, but he could never make a mistake as the reflection or being which is Love.

When Mrs. Eddy used the term Principle for God, she used the term that fully conveyed the idea of God. She wrote in *No and Yes*, "This Principle is Mind, substance, Life, Truth, Love. When understood, Principle is found to be the only term that fully conveys the ideas of God, — one Mind, a perfect man, and divine Science." There is a cause, a God. We see that we are ourselves. Therefore, there must be a Principle, since there can be no self-existence without a Principle. This means that there are laws by which this self-existence is continuously maintained, and this is the Science.

Mind's reflection or self-knowledge, which is going on

23

entirely within Mind as Mind, is the complete manifested presence we call man. Principle operates as effortless, spontaneous unfoldment, and this is the seed within itself, which multiplies and replenishes the earth. This is man, and it is God's proof of the continuity of His own self-existence.

John saw that Principle and its idea constitutes the one divine Being which can be called either God or man, depending from what standpoint one is speaking. When he said, "In the beginning [the Principle or cause] was the Word [idea] and the Word [idea] was with God [Mind] and the Word [idea] was God [Mind]." Man cannot be something that God is not, and God cannot be something that man is not; so if man as reflection were not Mind as its manifestation, man would be something that God is not, which would leave God without a knowledge of Himself and therefore a nonentity. God and man is like a single word, which when broken apart makes no sense.

Womanhood

The divine idea or Christ, unfolding the Fatherhood and sonship of God, appeared as the man Jesus, who in turn prophesied a greater than he, a Comforter, who would lead into all Truth. John the Revelator glimpsed the Comforter as a woman, typifying the spiritual idea of God's motherhood. *Science and Health* explains it this way, "As Elias presented the idea of the fatherhood of God, which Jesus afterwards manifested, so the Revelator completed this figure with woman, typifying the spiritual idea of God's motherhood."

In due course, this Comforter appeared as the revelation or creation where God is seen as the divine Principle, Love, embracing Life and Truth — Father and Son. Or to put it another way: this revelation of the Principle of Being as Life (Father), Truth (Son), Love (Mother) is the true idea or Comforter, the woman which leadeth into all Truth. It is interesting here to note that throughout human history the woman thought has always been the clearest transparency for Truth. The Bible record of the divine idea appearing through woman begins with Eve, who first recognized the impersonal nature of evil and continues to the vision of the Apocalypse. This revelation, or full Truth as the oneness of being unfolding as individual consciousness, naturally and inevitably was apprehended through or as a woman, Mary Baker Eddy. Her freedom from scholastic theology allowed the Christ idea to appear with no limitation of matter. God, as Principle and its idea, is the creator and creation, which is the one omnipotent, omnipresent, omniscient Being, of which Mrs. Eddy asks, "Was not this a revelation instead of a creation?" This spiritual fact, that being is one, that there is nothing outside or beside this conscious Mind, is the spiritual idea or Christ, which our textbook speaks of as being represented first by man and last by woman.

In an early edition of the textbook we have the statement that femininity gives the last, and therefore the highest idea of Deity. In our present edition we read, "The ideal woman corresponds to Life and to Love. In divine Science, we have not as much authority for considering God masculine, as we have for considering Him feminine, for Love imparts the clearest idea of Deity." This clear idea which Love imparts is the understanding that individual man is Mind's reflection of itself, an all-inclusive consciousness reflecting the creative Principle, "which reproduces the multitudinous forms of Mind." This clear perception of being frees mankind from any suggestion of want or impoverishment, since it is Father-Mother-Son reflected. This man embodies that which sustains or nourishes him and satisfies him.

This Christ idea typified by woman unfolds as the oneness of the male and female. The Revelator speaks of this idea or woman crowned with twelve stars, which the textbook says typifies the twelve tribes of Israel, which are all humanity. Thus we see the signification in our Leader's further statement that this woman symbolizes generic man, the individual reflection of Principle and idea as one Being. (See Revelation 17: 9-18.)

This immaculate idea clothed with the Sun (Spirit), as we have said before, is the true sense of Love, the Love which is Principle forever wedded to the expression of itself and this oneness is Soul and body, which is the acme of satisfaction and joy. This Love (Woman) conceives her man after the fullness of her own nature, which is Life, Truth and Love, (Father, Mother, Son), completeness — the full representation of Mind.

This man that is Love's immaculate conception, has dominion over all since he is all as Mind's infinite manifestation. This man is the sum of all substance, since Spirit can never be less than Spirit. He has no father and mother, and therefore is without beginning of years or end of days; and he has a better name than sons and daughters. Revelation records, "I Jesus have sent mine angel to testify unto you these things in the churches. I am the root and the offspring of David, and the bright and morning star." And in Isaiah we read, "Even unto them will I give in mine house and within my walls a place and a name better than of sons and of daughters: I will give them an everlasting name, that shall not be cut off." And, in *Miscellaneous Writings*, Mrs. Eddy phrases it this way, "I believe in God as the Supreme Being. I know not what the person of omnipotence and omnipresence is, or what the infinite includes; therefore, I worship that of which I can conceive, first, as a loving Father and Mother; then, as thought ascends the scale of being to diviner consciousness, God be-

comes to me, as to the apostle who declared it, 'God is Love,' —
divine Principle, — which I worship; and 'after the manner of my
fathers, so do I worship God.'"

Christ Science

What is the better name than sons and daughters of this
spiritual idea, this man which John the Revelator described as
a woman and whom Mrs. Eddy said was clad with the radiance
of Truth and with matter under her feet? It's name is *Christ
Science.* This spiritual idea, this Christ Science that has matter
under her feet, is the tree of Life, yielding her fruit every month
and whose leaves are for the healing of the nations. She is the
Holy City, the Kingdom of God, that the Revelator said he saw,
with no temple or body within it, but of which the Lord God Almighty (Principle) and the lamb (the spiritual idea of Love) were
the temple of it. In other words, "Principle and its idea is one, and
this one is God." A theologian has said "The light of the city of
God is Himself." The Kingdom of Heaven is Mind as infinite manifestation, and this is the male or female of its creation which is
revelation.

A definition of revelation is "immediate consciousness of
the real." This is creation or man. Man is not in the Kingdom of
Heaven, nor is the Kingdom of Heaven in man, but man *is* the
Kingdom of Heaven, the embodiment of all that is being. *Science
and Health* words it this way, "Jesus beheld in Science the perfect man, who appeared to him where sinning mortal man appears to mortals. In this perfect man the Saviour saw God's own
likeness, and this correct view of man healed the sick. Thus Jesus
taught that the kingdom of God is intact, universal, and that man is
pure and holy. Man is not a material habitation for Soul; he is
himself spiritual."

This Christ Science will eventually rule all nations and people, since it is Love embracing all nations and people as one Being. This understanding or idea is the male-female man, the womanhood of God, which remains to lead on the centuries.

The Christ Science, which is the male and female of God's creating, unfolds as the divine energy of Spirit, revealing newness of Life and the fulfillment of all desires; thus it wipes out human longing and striving and destroys all lust. "The serpent, material sense, will bite the heel of the woman, — will struggle to destroy the spiritual idea of Love; and the woman, this idea, will bruise the head of lust," *Science and Health* explains, while in *Miscellaneous Writings* we read, "It likewise silences all beliefs of opposition and friction and ends the conflict between the Spirit and the flesh," and "Truth said, and said from the beginning, 'Let us [Spirit] make man perfect;' and there is no other Maker: a perfect man would not desire to make himself imperfect, and God is not chargeable with imperfection. His modes declare the beauty of holiness, and His manifold wisdom shines through the visible world in glimpses of the eternal verities. Even through the mists of mortality is seen the brightness of His coming."

Science and Health further states, "This understanding of God as Love or divine Principle and idea is the full Truth which is God, and against this idea — the womanhood of God, the oneness of Being, the male and female man — the dragon cannot war." "The world must grow to the spiritual understanding of prayer. If good enough to profit by Jesus' cup of earthly sorrows, God will sustain us under these sorrows."

In this all-inclusive, immaculate consciousness, good no longer battles evil. To Love, all is Love, and our work as Christian Scientists is to live this Love that cannot conceive man with any capacity to do wrong, or suffer and die. The acme of Christian Science as our textbook reveals it, is that God, Spirit, creates all as in and of Himself, Spirit, and that this one universal male and female embodiment is forever unfolding its immaculateness as man and the universe, which you are.

Completeness

In considering this question of the manhood and womanhood of God, let us not think of a man and a woman, a male and a female. This unity or oneness of being does not mean the joining of a male to a female, nor of a man to a woman. There is relationship between ideas, for all is Mind and its infinite manifestation, and this is the only relationship. Therefore, Mind's reflection of itself is the one all-inclusive, indivisible consciousness of being, which is woman-man. The demonstration of the oneness of Principle and idea as individual consciousness might appear as what is called marriage and it might not, but it would mean perfect contentment and satisfaction, whether married or single.

The word *sex* is from two Latin words — *sexus*, meaning division, and *secare*, meaning to cut asunder. This immaculate idea, represented last by woman, is the idea of Love as Principle, which in doing away with the belief of duality, wipes out the belief of sex and reveals the wholeness and completeness of the one divine being as all-inclusive Life living itself.

This womanhood of God, unfolding as the complete satisfaction of Love with nothing left out of it, will bruise the head of lust. Sex is the belief of disunity, of duality whenever disunity is seen. The one divine Being cannot be divided, and the belief that it is divided or cut asunder, is sex. Thus we see war as an aspect of sex, a belief of division or cutting asunder. It is a belief of lust, which is always a longing for satisfaction and completeness, and a fear of lack and impoverishment, always a longing to get something, always a fear that it cannot be gotten.

Let us know, "I am this manhood manifesting or showing forth as my own divine being all that God or Mind is unfolding of His own infinite perfection. I am manifesting that supreme joy and contentment which human sense interprets as a beautiful home, a happy family, love and affluence without measure. Beauty, wholeness, and completeness do not require a medium or a process to be Mind. Every manifestation which I behold is an idea of God, manifested as my conscious being or individual consciousness. The manifestation of Mind in all its perfect beauty, wholeness, loveliness, is what I am. I am not conscious of something, but the something I seem to behold is my consciousness, is the true I or us (Mind). Infinity means there is now nothing outside of itself. Mind is the awareness or consciousness which constitutes what we call things." We read in *Science and Health*, "The life of man is Mind."

The understanding that consciousness is existence insures the indestructibility and permanence of what is called our universe, whether it is nation or friend. When this Mind which is Love, our Mind, looks out from itself to itself and reflects its own perfection, its universality, harmony and joy, this is your Kingdom of Heaven (yourself) peopled with divine ideas. Let us not think there is anything "out there," any lovely trait, or character, or beautiful or harmonious surroundings, which we do not seem to have, since it seems to belong personally to someone else. Character is not personal, nor is beauty or joy. Such thinking is a denial of God as All and as our own infinite individuality as reflection. This is having other gods, other good, before Me, the one I or Ego.

Whatever confronts us as something to do or something to be done, since it is a part of consciousness, must be understood as Mind. All consciousness is Mind. What we apparently do or shall we say be, is in Science the well doing or well being of Mind, forever unfolding. If we are sailing a boat, Science enables us to disregard the sense picture and believe only what we understand; and that is, that the apparent physical activity which we behold is Mind, never person or matter. Before what to our present sense of seeming was called sailing a boat, is Mind looking out from its own infinitude and beholding its joyous, free, effortless activity. Therefore man, including sailing the boat, is the harmonious unfoldment of Mind. In understanding that Mind is the performer always and man the performance, we demonstrate ease, joy and freedom, regardless of what the task may seem to be. Since man is the evidence of Mind's activity, he does not sail a boat, but he and the sailing of the boat are one harmonious unfoldment of Mind. If one were confronted with a task to be performed, understanding that Mind is the performer always, and never man, we demonstrate ease, joy and freedom in the performance, since as the evidence of Mind's performing, we are the performance.

It is a common mistake to think of spirituality in terms of morality. Morality is only spirituality when it ceases to be associated with materiality. Study the definition of moral on page 115 of *Science and Health*: "MORAL. Humanity, honesty, affection, compassion, hope, faith, meekness, temperance." The marginal heading, "Transitional qualities," shows that the moral qualities are evil beliefs disappearing and the perception of spiritual ideas. Moral qualities have no value in themselves from any spiritual standpoint when they seem to appear in human beings. Moral qualities must not be associated with material persons. Let us understand this and we will no longer waste our time in trying to be good, develop good in our character. Instead we will bend every effort to understand God in the light of Science. This understanding will appear to human sense as good character and morals. To associate these moral qualities with a mortal is to associate them with disintegration and death.

Malpractice

I should like to say something here about malpractice. We have used this word a great deal of the time indiscriminately and incorrectly. Malpractice is the belief that man is a person with a personal mind, so that any indulgence of this belief is malpractice. Any thought of man as person, either with good or bad qualities, is malpractice. All gossip, since it discusses persons and tends to deny the oneness of being, is malpractice. Does this affect the person discussed? No, except as it constitutes his belief about himself. But it does affect the person discussing another, since he is discussing his own false concept of being, and this dulls his perception of real being. Your wrong thoughts of others constitute a part of what seems to be yourself, since you have identified yourself with the belief that man is a person. When you accept the belief of a mind apart from God, this constitutes your malpractice upon yourself and not your neighbor's malpractice upon you.

Since to each one the only consciousness is the one claiming to be his own, it is evident that what seems to be another's opposition to us is actually our opposition to them. Opposition is the anti-Christ, and the anti-Christ is the belief that we are persons. Mortal mind, seeing duality, sees its vices in contradiction to its virtues, and this appears as personal good and personal evil. It is obvious that there can be no opposition when there is the understanding that Mind is one, both noumenon and phenomena. We can feel no opposition when we have no persons in our thought.

32

Malpractice cannot produce a result. That which appears as a result is the belief of malpractice itself. The textbook explains it this way: "The fact that pain cannot exist where there is no mortal mind to feel it is a proof that this so-called mind makes its own pain — that is, its own *belief* in pain." What asks the question "What is evil?" The question itself asks the question. The belief and the believer are one, and this one is illusion. *Malpractice*

 Let us recognize that the uncovering of a false belief claiming to be personal belief, is but the uncovering of a false collective or universal belief which has always existed, as the lie about Truth is never personal or private. This false collective belief is actually breaking up when it is brought to light or it would not appear in conscious thought. Therefore, we understand that while the breaking up of material belief may seem to be this or that, what is actually occurring is Truth appearing and error disappearing, since all that can be going on is the reality of all things.

 Since consciousness is one, both in belief and in fact, what seems to be the subjective state of one's own thought is the subjective state of another's thought. There is no private mortal or human mind. The physical world is made up of the conscious and unconscious thoughts of mortals. The collective belief of the world constitutes what is called the carnal human mind. One is free from the false beliefs which seem to constitute one's present sense of the universe through spiritual education alone, which is instruction in Divine Science. Never for an instant think you are protected from the belief of evil because you personally do not entertain any phase of belief in evil as your conscious thought. So long as the belief of evil claims to be conscious thought of anyone, it has conscious identity in belief; and therefore, in order to defend one's self from its suggestions, one must consciously think what is true, constantly identify one's self with God. All error is the result of wrong identification.

The human mind cannot shut out a false mental picture. So your endeavor to shut out a false belief by refusing to read the daily paper or to consider in any way what appears as the collective belief of the world, is of no value.

You demonstrate your individuality, which is your defense, by identifying yourself with the divine Mind. Naturally this identification is easier when one's thought is not constantly assailed with the false picture, but one must learn to identify one's self with God in the midst of seeming evil. To those instructed in Science to look out from Mind with no other outlook, what appears to human sense as nations at war, friends in conflict, indicates the unreality and consequent disappearance of that which is false and the reappearing of that which never was absent.

Individuality

What seems to be individuality in mortal mind is simply its own self-division expressed as material persons and material things. All individuality or identity in its infinite variety is the one indivisible Being — Mind as infinite manifestation, the I AM THAT I AM. In *Miscellaneous Writings* we find this question, "Who wants to be mortal, or would not gain the true ideal of Life and recover his own individuality?"

Since man is compound idea including all right ideas, generic man is an aspect of individual man. When one gives identity to the belief that man is a person, this deceptive sense appears to separate God and man, and this robs man of his individuality. The human concept called person is a misstatement of the divine idea. ". . . the human concept antagonizes the divine." (ibid)

Since being is one, war, conflict, disease, is a lie about unity of being. When one gives identity to the belief that man is a person, this is his separation from God and results in antagonism and warfare. In Mrs. Eddy's *Retrospection and Introspection* we read, "God reflects Himself, or Mind, but does not subdivide Mind, or good, into minds, good and evil. Divine Science demands mighty wrestlings with mortal beliefs, as we sail into the eternal haven over the unfathomable sea of possibilities."

The minute there are two, a human and a divine in our world picture, there is friction, antagonism, conflict. This antagonism is not actually a warfare between two things, but is antagonism which must necessarily exist between that which is and the false view of it. It is a supposed warfare between the personal sense of being and the divine idea or entity of being. It is the belief that Mind and its infinite manifestation, although acknowledged to be God, and therefore one being, includes within Himself the finite concept which naturally opposes Himself.

The reason for our difficulty is the belief that Mind and its infinite manifestation, although acknowledged to be God, and therefore one being, includes as a part of being the finite concept of itself. Existence is consciousness, and since consciousness is one because it is Mind, God, it is not divided nor divisible, and cannot include anything that opposes or antagonizes. It cannot include anything that is in opposition to itself.

Treatment

Since man has no Mind but God, letting that Mind be your Mind, knowing that it is *All*, constitutes your defense from every accusation of the carnal mind. This knowing is divine power. Evil cannot assert itself in any way except as belief. You cannot send a good thought or an evil thought. There is no transference of thought. Divine thought cannot be transferred, since Mind operates by virtue of its omnipresence. One's understanding of being determines the way his universe appears to him, since we are always dealing with our spiritual perceptions and not with the things which we perceive; we are always dealing with the Truth as it unfolds to us individually. Therefore one person cannot give another person any advice, or determine for another the right course to pursue. I cannot outline for you what your spiritual vision will reveal to you. Mind does that. I can know the Truth and present to you the facts of being, but I cannot outline how that Truth will appear to you. Mind does that.

Mrs. Eddy speaks of the spiritual determining the outward and actual. One cannot be spiritually minded for another, and therefore cannot determine what the outward appearance would be. Any advice one would give another from the standpoint of his own spiritual vision would dull the perception of the one taking the advice and limit his demonstration.

Each one must act from the highest standpoint of his own spiritual vision or understanding. The work of Christian Science is to free the human race from the false theology that divides the one divine being into beings, separating God and man, and to heal the sick and straighten out our disordered lives. The student of Christian Science is no more personally responsible for what is called healing than the student of mathematics for the correction of an error in a mathematical problem. The principle of mathematics illustrates its own unwavering law through the understanding of the mathematician. What appears to the so-called human sense to be the healing of persons and things, is that we are no longer deceived by the belief of life in matter.

All healing in Christian Science is the operation of divine Principle as the understanding of the Christian Scientist. Thinking what is true, which is Truth expressing itself, constitutes Science

in its activity. Healing, or apparent improvement of what is called
the human being, does not mean any change in the human being. It
means that when being is understood as divine, it is actually seen
in that degree. The unseen appears as the seen through the understanding of what actually is, since the health, happiness and affluence of what appears to be human existence is entirely in Mind,
and is demonstrated as the consciousness of each one. We look
within to find reality, the divine identity of all that appears to us as
matter. What appears as a human being is actually man — divine
in being. Any healing which may seem to be accomplished on any
other basis than the unreality of matter is not Christian Science
healing, but is some phase of mental suggestion endeavoring to
change a mental or a physical phenomenon.

The denial in Christian Science of the reality of the false
human mind and the insistence that nothing exists but the infinite
and harmonious Mind, destroys the lie that disease or limitation is
anything but the deception called matter. The human mind is de-
liberately used as a factor for healing in mental science practice,
but the human mind is the reason for disease in Christian Science
practice, since mortal mind and matter are one. Mistaken treat-
ment is exposed in *Science and Health*, "Such theories have no
relationship to Christian Science, which rests on the conception
of God as the only Life, substance, and intelligence, and excludes
the human mind as a spiritual factor in the healing work."

What we are dealing with is perception and not a thing
perceived. The argument — that happiness, pleasure, health, com-
panionship are expressed through matter and are something one
gains through change of thought — has claimed to dull the spiritual perception of many a Christian Scientist. "We are Christian
Scientists, only as we quit our reliance upon that which is false
and grasp the true. We are not Christian Scientists until we leave

37

all for Christ. Human opinions are not spiritual. They come from the hearing of the ear, from corporeality instead of from Principle, and from the mortal instead of from the immortal. Spirit is not separate from God." (ibid) Demonstration must not be associated with material or personal possessions.

When material sense testifies to the adjustment of circumstances which bring happiness or the achievement of wealth through doing away with worry and fear, we have been accustomed to call these changes proofs of Christian Science. This type of thing is dangerous since it assures duality of Mind and is mental science, the direct antithesis of Christian Science. It is only as one understands health, wealth and happiness as something one is aware of as an unfoldment of Mind, that he is disposed to cease clinging to the human concepts. Again in the textbook Mrs. Eddy tells us, "The determination to hold spirit in the grasp of matter is the persecutor of Truth and Love."

Christian Science cannot really be called a method of salvation. Christian Science is really the revelation that there is nothing to be saved. Spiritual consciousness is divine understanding. It is not a development or improvement of the human mind. Truth is not a tool to destroy error, since error's seeming is only the hidden existence of good. Error cannot be destroyed since it has no being, and is only a misinterpretation of the fact.

A laboratory or formulas do not make a chemist. Just so as to a Christian Scientist. He is not made by using statements of Truth to deny evil and affirm good, what is actually called "working to destroy error." He is made by understanding the basic premise of Christian Science, that God is one, and therefore *All*, and that there is no error.

A Christian Scientist is not knowing the truth to bring about harmony, since harmony is already the law of all being, nor is he concerned over what appears to him as error. He knows that today Truth appears to human sense as the uncovering and disappearing of false concepts; and the more violent the error, the more rapid its disappearance; so his whole effort is spent in the endeavor to dematerialize his sense of Spirit so that his substance will be unmolested in the chemicalization. This spiritual cultivation of thought which Christian Science provides, enables him to rejoice in spite of the picture. Joy in the fact that Principle is invincible, begets a courage based on Truth, which is not a development of human character, but is the disappearance of fear. We cannot outline the way in which Truth is appearing and how error, fulfilling the condition of its own nothingness, will disappear to human sense. We know there is nothing to save or be saved.

Christian Science interprets the divine Principle called God, and saves the sinner and heals the sick by dissipating the belief that there is a sinner and a sick man. The understanding and practice of Christian Science by the individual constitutes a Christian Scientist, and is the Christ Science which is the healing presence and power of God among men because it is the true man.

What is called salvation is understanding, righteous knowing, and this is healing. It is giving up the so-called human mind and knowing its correction. The practitioner may seem to be working for a patient, but really he is demonstrating his own perfection. Since being is one, in freeing himself from the suggestion of mortality, the false mental picture that there is life and presence other than infinite good, he demonstrates the perfection of his so-called patient. His own knowing is the patient knowing, since this knowing is really Truth expressing itself and appearing as his patient, effacing the false evidence of discord if the patient is ready to give up the false belief. In the case of the woman with issue of blood, Jesus relied on his own understanding, or Christ, and this appeared to human sense as the working of miracles.

One must be alert to every suggestion that good is absent. The effort to reject your own supposititious materiality is prayer without ceasing. This suggestion that good is absent may come up as a patient, or as the temperamental characteristics of what is called yourself, or it may come as war. To the real metaphysician the form in which this suggestion appears is of no importance. What is important is that this seeming absence of good is claiming to be his own individual consciousness, even when it seems to be a patient or a war; and because it is claiming to be his consciousness, he can do something about it. One is wasting time when one considers the lie in any way, or seeks to find an answer to the problem, or the cause of the problem in the problem.

One cannot enter a dream and find out why a lion is chasing the dreamer or do anything about the lion. One must remember that the picture confronting us is returning to us what purports to be our picture, or the image which claims to be ourselves. In belief we are always dealing with the thing perceived, so the good and evil we seem to perceive is in the perception. If one is entertaining a concept of being, a mental picture that includes age, poverty, hate, etc., then the age, poverty and hate which you believe to be someone else, is you in belief, since you have identified yourself with the belief, and "the belief and the believer are one."

One may be thinking all that is true about one's self; but if you believe that someone else is thinking or expressing that which is not true, you are doing that false thinking yourself. If you see anything as material, you are seeing your own belief in materiality. So when you have a patient — you are your patient. If you have a war, you are your war. When this point is clear to the student, he realizes that in working out his own salvation he is doing all he can for his brother man or the world. There is no greater love and, therefore, no greater potency than laying down a material sense of life that attempts to dull your vision. This is the love which sees the manifestation of God within your own mind as the reality of all that seems to confront you, and in so seeing, you demonstrate the one God-Being as your own being.

So the only good I can see is the good which I am as Mind's reflection. The good is never "out there" as person, place, or thing. Eternity is the timeless experience of good. We can only call that good which helps free from the bondage of matter. Personal good is a prison. Actual good, which is God, lives outside of personal sense. The good which one thinks resides in person, place, or thing does not reside there; but is the good which is reflected of God, and is everywhere present even when it is covered up by the belief that man is a good person. Any attempt to make a person happy in matter, any act that keeps our brother in bondage of matter or personal sense, is not good, no matter what ease or joy it seems to bring.

Charity

One may have to do something for someone who seems less fortunate than one's self, but you can let the one who disperses charity think on that level of belief, since the thinking which accepts poverty is poverty itself. The good which one thinks he is doing because of someone's need is evil, because it identifies his brother man, which is also himself, with this suppositional mind that is wholly illusion, and thus with disintegration and death. One's actions are always from the standpoint of the "better belief," but one thinks always from the standpoint of Mind, and never on the basis of belief.

Jesus acted as if there were sick people, but he thought from the standpoint of Truth and knew that God and man are one being. Any concession one may have to make to the improved belief must be seen as an indication of ignorance of what is truly being, since when one knows better, knows what is true, one will see more clearly what is true. In this picture, this improved belief, there will be less poverty, less war, less sickness, and gradually we will not be called upon to help anyone on the basis of the belief.

We have been educated to judge the good and evil of what is called human experience by an ideal. We have ideals of human conduct and human thinking, not recognizing that a human ideal is really personal sense. Any endeavor to outline God, or good, in the realm of the human, will keep us from demonstrating the good which is God, which is unfoldment as Mind. What seems to be the unselfishness of a person is more often than not a projection of self more devastating than what is called selfishness, since no one is tempted to call selfishness good, but almost everyone is tempted to call unselfishness the devotion to a human idea, which is the building up of a personal self-good. So long as one does anything, no matter how commendable from any standpoint except that of pure Spirit, he is serving other gods and is making unto himself a graven image. We must not work up to God from the standpoint of the belief, but from God down to the belief. Personal unselfishness is not a liberation from personal sense, but a form of idolatry.

One may appear to be brave, strong, generous, loyal, self-sacrificing, and yet be demonstrating none of the righteousness of Principle. Many human beings are what is called "good" because they have never been tempted. We are idolatrous when we deal with the world objectively — that is, when we consider our possessions as matter and react to their stimulation either of pleasure or of pain. Do not misunderstand me, the courage, the

generosity, the joy, the loyalty, the self-sacrifice, all the so-called Christian virtues that our Leader calls transitional qualities are some discernment of that which is true; but when misinterpreted as belonging to the human being to be cultivated as something good, these so-called virtues become vices, since any personality of good is a denial of God. Achievement on the level of the human belief is always evil, and we are wasting our time in trying to transform evil into good. Good is forever unknowable by the human mind. There can be no good in the realm of human belief. There are only different degrees of evil. Therefore, we must follow the instruction of our textbook — "We must leave the mortal basis of belief and unite with the one Mind" — if we are to demonstrate the good which is changeless. We can demonstrate good only where good is — in Mind as Mind.

The difference between good and evil is not the difference between a good thing and a bad thing, but is entirely a difference in appearance or viewpoint. The flat earth and the sphere were the same object, the difference lay in the viewpoint. One never existed, the other antedated every ignorant concept.

Personalizing Good

They said to Jesus, "Good Master, What shall I do that I may inherit eternal life?" and Jesus said, "Why callest thou me good? there is none good but one and that is God." Jesus did not answer this question directly, but asked a question himself, which seemed to be a rebuke, but actually it was an answer to their question. Their first step in knowing about eternal life was to see that it had nothing to do with personal good. The goodness which we think we see, is the goodness which is found in Mind expressed in the individual consciousness. There is nothing outside of Truth and its expression. The chief problem of the human race is in personalizing good, which is personal worship. It is in the religious world that one most often finds the personalization of good in some group or individual. That this danger would present itself to the Christian Scientists, Mrs. Eddy explained in her article "Personal Contagion," found on page 116 of *Miscellany*.

The disintegrating effects of a blind obedience to a person are expressed by Jesus when he said that if the blind lead the blind both will fall into the ditch. Today the devotion to a dogma, the zealous adherence to form, the tendency to accept the concept of denominationalism is claiming to sap the vital efficiency and spiritual aims of the Christian Science movement, just as it has sapped reformatory movements down through the centuries.

The apathy observable in our movement does not mean that Christian Scientists love Christian Science less, but as a class they are doing less individual thinking. Whenever and wherever this happens, it is the dullness and inertia of mortal mind. The conformity to some letter of authoritative statement, without understanding the Spirit, is a dead thing. "It is the Spirit that quickenith; the flesh profiteth nothing." To deny a personal teacher and recognize the impersonal Teacher or Christ, involves one in a denial of all selfhood apart from God. This is the demand upon us if the Christian Science movement is to prosper. Personal sense is rebuked in this statement from *Science and Health*, "The student who receives his knowledge of Christian Science or metaphysical healing from a human teacher, may be mistaken in judgment and demonstration, but God cannot mistake." Is fearful loyalty to an individual teacher or group the basis for individual demonstration of Principle?

Human good can never destroy evil, since it requires evil in the form of personality in order to be good, and it is this evil and good which comprises personality. "Self love is more opaque than a solid body," and the love we think we have for another person is really love for ourselves; therefore, this love would blind our eyes to the error which might be destroying us. Personal love is no better than personal hate, and as we have said many times, it is really worse since it makes hypocrites of people. They think they are something which they are not. Jesus said, "Except your righteousness exceeds the righteousness of the scribes and Pharisees ye shall not enter the Kingdom of Heaven."

The scribes and Pharisees of Jesus' time were the best citizens, the good people. No evil is so evil as the evil that calls itself good. It was the personalization of the Christ in the worship of Jesus, Mary's son, which so dulled the vision that for generations the Christ was a theory and not a practical presence.

The Christ could have never reappeared as Christian Science if the Christ had ever been confined to the personal Jesus, Let us consider Jesus as our understanding of what he was. Constantly denying the sense of himself as Jesus, he embodied the Christ. "I am the way, the Truth and the Life." There was no false humility or miserable sinner about him, and no sense that he was a person, either bad or good, but rather the pure consciousness of his inseparable oneness with God.

Words

Exercise care in your use of words. Do not use words or phrases perfunctorily or mechanically, simply because they seem to be accepted as Christian Science phraseology. The student of Christian Science must be alert in his use of language since words are the expression of thought. If words are used without intelligence, "they become as sounding brass and tinkling symbols."

When we turn to divine Mind, the ideas or understanding which are that Mind in expression, will find words to make them live. The Christ which Jesus understood himself to be, demonstrated its presence in just such words. As Jesus said, "My words shall not pass away," which means, "My ideas or understanding will not pass away." This was likewise true of Mary Baker Eddy. The discovery of Christian Science was an impersonal attainment. It is the Christ consciousness which demonstrates the words and phrases which awaken the thought to ideas. The words and phrases do not create the ideas, but the ideas create the words. As our understanding unfolds, the meaning of the words will constantly unfold. A stock phrase repeated as a matter of form or habit does not constitute an understanding of Truth. Taking the words of an inspired writer and quoting them, does not constitute the understanding which heals the sick, for it is the action of mortal mind only. Mind manifests itself as ideas, and since they are the one idea in its infinity of variety, these ideas cannot be humanly confined in a set group of phrases.

The only reason one ever speaks or writes of the Truth, or uses words, is that thought may perceive the Truth that seems to be unfolding only in the consciousness of the speaker or the writer, but which really is Truth itself unfolding as the consciousness of all. Because these ideas are actually Mind unfolding as the universal consciousness, words needed to reveal these ideas of God as the consciousness of all, must be Mind demonstrating itself. Truth is revealed as individual consciousness; revelator is only incidental to the human sense of things. When one says, "Divine Love always has met and always will meet every human need," the idea which these words express must be spiritual — if divine Love meets the human need. The human need is not for a piano, a dress, or food, but for divine Love. Divine Love does not give us a rent check or food, but manifests itself as the pure vision or consciousness which includes all good and sees its own manifestation everywhere. This Love entertains no personal prejudices, no recognition of either good or evil as belonging to a human being. Love sees nothing to criticize or condemn.

Gratitude

Gratitude is a word used so emotionally as to be practically meaningless a great deal of the time. Gratitude is a wonderful word when understood, and about the most hypocritical and useless word when not understood. When not understood it becomes simply an intensity of human emotion. Frequently it is used to express gratitude to personalities, to the practitioner, or to Mrs. Eddy. Let us analyze its meaning from the standpoint of Principle. Since man is only a term to express God's unfoldment of His own nature and character, God cannot cease unfolding what man is, since man is what God is. Then Love, Truth, good, etc. is no gift from God to man, but is the divine order of Being. Then why be grateful to God, when man is just as important to God as God is to man. An understanding of the Love which is never separate from its manifestation is true being, and this dissipates the belief that being is mortal and therefore limited and finite. Then what is the true idea which the word gratitude expresses?

In the idea of acknowledgement, recognition or appreciation, God recognizes Himself as All. He appreciates Himself as all good, as all Truth. In the ratio that your thinking approximates the divine Mind, recognizing and appreciating all that apparently confronts you as Mind's expression of its goodness and loveliness, you are being grateful, and all your words of gratitude for material things are dead, since the true idea is absent. The minute

47

I am grateful for material things, for expression of Love on the part of friends and family, etc., I am making unto myself a graven image and am bowing down and serving it. The love that I see expressed, is the love which is God, and is never expressed by person to persons, although that is what appears to human sense when divine Love is demonstrated as the Principle of being.

True Government

All that lives must have a Principle or law for its living. What God creates He must necessarily maintain and unfold, or God would be without a witness or proof of His own eternality. The creative Principle is not only creative, but is that which keeps creation going in perfect harmony and order. This Principle in operation is what is known as government. The word government in its accepted sense implies a governor and a governed based on the belief of a universe peopled with many beings whose recipients are more or less in conflict. Hence the necessity of working out a system whereby these different viewpoints may be used constructively for the good of all. The problems of so-called government cannot be solved until the interests of the individual and the interests of the state are seen to be one.

There are three forms of so-called government: (1) government by the church, by a personal representative of God, such as a Pope or any church heirachy set up as authority. This type of government is called Theocracy; *Theo* means God. (2) Government by the state. This is called autocracy. *Auto* meaning self; Monarchy comes under this classification with its divine right of Kings. (3) Government by the people for the people, one for all and all for one. This is called Democracy.

Theos, *autos* and *demos* combined with *cracy* derived

from the verb *stratum*, means to rule and signify rule by God, rule by self, rule by the people; this is the false rule. Therefore, in any effort to demonstrate a satisfying, satisfactory government, we must begin with an understanding of the universality of being. In this understanding one finds no self-interests since being is one. What is thought to be thy neighbor is simply a fuller expression of the one true selfhood or reflection which is thyself. This is clearly stated in *Science and Health*: "'Thou shalt have no other gods before me.' (Exodus xx. 3.) The First Commandment is my favorite text. It demonstrates Christian Science. It inculcates the tri-unity of God, Spirit, Mind; it signifies that man shall have no other spirit or mind but God, eternal good, and that all men shall have one Mind. The divine Principle of the First Commandment bases the Science of being, by which man demonstrates health, holiness, and life eternal. One infinite God, good, unifies men and nations; constitutes the brotherhood of man; ends wars; fulfils the Scripture, 'Love thy neighbor as thyself;' annihilates pagan and Christian idolatry, — whatever is wrong in social, civil, criminal, political, and religious codes; equalizes the sexes; annuls the curse on man, and leaves nothing that can sin, suffer, be punished or destroyed."

In an early edition of our textbook we find these words, "This Science of being alone enables us to love God with all our heart and our neighbor as ourselves." Our textbook says that there must be willingness to leave the false landmarks and joy to see them disappear and that this disposition helps to precipitate the ultimate harmony. Many times it is difficult to rejoice or be willing when we see the old concepts disappear while the vision of the new is still dim. It is only when those concepts not only fail to satisfy, but are oppressive and tyrannical that we turn from them with joy. Truth cannot appear in a consciousness clouded by tradition. Therefore, before the Christ idea could appear in its full effulgence, mankind had to turn resolutely from false concepts of Church and state which were so blinding.

Throughout the ages this divine idea, this Christ, the Science of being, has acted as the impulsion continually forcing the disappearance of the false concepts in order that man may know his God aright, and find in that knowing that God is present with him as all good, as his very own consciousness. The rebellion against tradition and a man-interpreted God, which was expressed by the Church of Rome, was called in human history the Reformation. Later this was followed by the Puritan movement in England, rebelling against the inhibitions and prohibitions of the English Church which had become as demanding as the Roman church before it. This rebellion against the church also coincided with the rebellion against imperialism, and the right of the people to govern themselves began to unfold in thought. As this understanding process went on, some gleam of democracy appeared and one of the results of the reform was the creation of the United States of America, the first real democracy, since it is a republic.

This virgin consciousness liberated from imperialism, as well as scholastic and state theology, declared its freedom thus: "That all men are created equal; among these are life, liberty and the pursuit of happiness; that to insure these rights, governments are instituted among men deriving their just powers from the consent of the governed." The consent of the governed makes the governed its own governor. Was not this some glimpse of the fact that being is one, and therefore that self-government is God government?

This one divine being is Principle and idea reflected as man and the universe; therefore, democracy in its true meaning is one as all and all as one. This is an idea and not a system of human government. This perception of the infinite individuality of being, faint as it was, presaged the reappearing of the Christ as an impersonal Science of a nation, which while one, and functioning as one, is composed of units, each functioning as one. Our forefathers had seen the failure of personal domination and were actually seeking, through impartial establishment of impersonal good, the good which is the heritage of everyone.

The true constitution of anything is not only its inherent character, which goes to make it up, but it is also the authority and law under which it functions; in short, the constitution of anything is its Principle. That which constitutes these United States of America is the Love which is Principle unfolding the oneness of being as the individual consciousness, and appearing as equality of opportunity to and for all men. Under constitution the freedom, joy and dominion of the individual is guaranteed. Since this constitution is divinely ordained, its utility to live and bless all nations and peoples, its unassailableness, appears in the ratio of our understanding of what constitutes true being, the Kingdom of Heaven as man.

We have not inherited a constitution, but we *are* the constitution forever unfolding the inseparableness of God and man. Spiritually understood these United States is not a nation, but a state of consciousness, unfolding the individuality of being which is universal being. When the impersonal Christ was no longer obscured by the mist of dogma and tradition, and true Christianity had gained a foothold in human consciousness, the Science of Christianity appeared. By all that had preceded it, the human consciousness was prepared for this immaculate conception of Christian Science. Thus the Saviour from the tyranny and opposition of the belief that man is other than God's manifestation of Himself, became operative in what is called human experience by redeeming consciousness. Since the formation of this government illustrates the coincidence of the human and the divine, or the working of the Christ, the spiritual idea, in consciousness, all nations must come to this nation to be saved. This Christ or spiritual idea says, "All must come to the Father by me." As in olden time they came to Jesus, now they come to where this idea of man's true individuality is appearing. Multitudes followed Jesus. Why? Because he knew man's individual oneness with God made him the Christ.

What we know individually of the unity of being is our Christ and will draw all men unto us. Let us remember that the Principle of self-government (one for all, all for one) is practical and demonstrable when it is understood that man cannot be divided into men or nations. Man or nation exist as compound idea, including all right ideas. The demonstration of right from the standpoint of Truth cannot result in friction and disunity. It is only when thought is based on the human sense of right, which is always wrong, that friction and disunity can appear.

Civilization is that state of consciousness where a true understanding of God determines the viewpoint of its people. A so-called civilization, where mere tradition and precedent determinates viewpoint, cannot survive, and no matter how much effort is expended in attempting to preserve such a civilization, we will see it crumble before our eyes. This crumbling is not the destruction of anything real, but rather the destruction of a system of thinking which must pass away. In fact, it is as a false sense disappears that reality can appear. True civilization is the culture resulting from spiritual enlightenment, and there is no other civilization. This culture consists of a knowledge of God which reveals man as His manifestation. With the marginal note "Useful knowledge" in *Science and Health* we read "The point for each one to decide is, whether it is mortal mind or immortal Mind that is causative. We should forsake the basis of matter for metaphysical Science and its divine Principle."

True Progress

Thinking in terms of personality and matter must give way completely to reasoning on the basis of Principle. It is this true knowledge of God which reveals that the anti-Christ is not only what is considered by the world to be paganism, but is any concept of God which includes the reality of matter or evil, or a man needing to be saved or healed.

The great impediment to progress is the state of consciousness which personalizes good and evil. When Principle removes what mortal mind calls foundational, mortal mind is left without anything on which to build. This is what we call chaos. So long as humanity continues to identify itself with matter, the chaotic picture will continue, since mortal mind can only prove its nothingness by the ceaseless seeming destruction of itself, in obedience to the immutable law of Spirit.

Until one becomes fully aware that it is the Mind which is God which is functioning as Mind, he is in the darkness even when he thinks he is in the light of Truth. Truth is Truth — it is not human opinion. Truth will force humanity to become dissatisfied with its man-made God, its man-made religion. A ready-made religion is nothing better than pagan idolatry, since it is largely the acceptance of another's creed or experience.

The looking to a leader or a group, or to a concept of God or good built up out of established orthodox beliefs, dulls our perception of true being, the oneness of God and man. The knowledge of this oneness is the Christ or Christian Science, which comes by individual revelation, the consciousness of each one of us, and thus destroys incarnate error. How, then, can there be any person or group to aid us in forming our opinion, no matter what position they may seem to occupy in the world or in our Christian Science movement? To do so is to deny Mind's individual demonstration of the Christ, a denial of the oneness which is self-government, which is God's government. No practitioner or teacher of Christian Science should attempt to act as a substitute for the understanding of the individual. Mrs. Eddy says, "Follow me only so far as I follow Christ," which is tantamount to saying, "Follow the revelation, know the Truth with me, not because of me." A leader is only incidental to the human sense of things, and it is a false theology to believe that obedience to any human leader ensures one's salvation.

When we look for any direction outside of our spiritual thinking, we are not demonstrating the oneness of Principle and idea as our own selfhood. One cannot understand and thus demonstrate the oneness of being vicariously. There is only one Christ infinitely manifested as individual man, but as one attempts to make his own an understanding of God which is another's, by following in another's human steps, the Christ is absent for that one. We can never demonstrate divine reflection by holding as our goal what another did or does. Christian Science cannot be demonstrated intellectually. Blind obedience to another's demonstration of oneness does not insure protection against the belief of evil.

Christian Science demonstration is purely a spiritual activity unfolding as individual understanding. Mind alone demonstrates Science. It has nothing to do with person or things. Mrs. Eddy wrote the textbook for Christians, not for sinners. "The healthy sinner is the hardened sinner," she said. Therefore, until one is sufficiently awakened to be dis-eased in the belief of being a mortal, he is not ready to give up a human sense of self that Christian Science demands. As Christian Scientists, we are engaged in a scientific work and must give up Christian theories, which do not heal the sick. Christianity must be a Science or there is no true Christianity. Jesus' demonstration of Spirit vanquished human selfhood and matter.

Just as Mrs. Eddy wrote her book for Christians, so the first appeal of Christian Science to a newcomer is usually to his religious instinct and convictions. This appeal, while it may have results that are encouraging and helpful, is eventually found inadequate to meet the demands of the Science of Christianity.

Anyone discerning even faintly the great truths of Christian Science cannot fail to see the inevitable disappearance of satisfaction and comfort in believing in personal selfhood and matter as substance. Methods of government and methods of directing industry, even though based on high ideals, will seem to fail for the simple reason that people must look to God, to Spirit, not to personality or matter. When one sees what he has been educated to call his world topple before his eyes, dismay, fear, insecurity and doubt rise up to torment him. This dismay and despair is a good sign, since when forced into a narrow enough space or against a blank wall, one will have to look up and then will see the angel.

There is always an angel, a still small voice saying, "Do not be alarmed at this seeming revolution, but let go. Do not try to save or heal anything. Do not identify yourself with the seeming picture. Do not hold on to that concept which has seemed so real, so enjoyable, so satisfying, but has limited and hampered you since it has clouded your vision of reality."

The more of good the mortal concept seems to possess, the more it clouds our vision. This letting go of the human picture is absolutely essential, since the contemplation of the picture in any of its aspects identifies us with it. It is the pure in heart that see God.

True Citizenship

The joining of welfare organizations and cooperation in so-called social betterment plans and institutional work are not necessarily indicative of good citizenship. One may or may not join in any such activity as a result of a clearer vision of what is actually going on. What one appears to "do" is entirely the human appearing of the knowledge of the Truth which one has. These human activities are largely palliative; in fact, they are entirely so when considered from the standpoint of the human need. Anything that one does from within the deceptive sense of the problem is really of no value in solving the problem. The suggestion that one needs to "do something" to bring about a state of affairs is part of the suggestion that there is a world in trouble. Let us rid ourselves of the suggestion that there is actually such a world, and then we will "do," without human planning, whatever seems necessary to make that fact apparent to all. No matter what seems helpful to human sense, it is not helpful unless the help is understood to be of divinity — the actual appearing of the perfection that is interpreted as indispensable human footsteps leading to perfection. Then what appeared to be doing something to bring a more perfect state is understood in Science to be perfection itself being individual consciousness. It is Love appearing in a form to meet what is called a human need. It is easier to rush about smartly and clean the outside of the platter — in other words, "do" something, rather than "know" or "be" something — not realizing that we will "do" right if we "be" or "know" what is Truth. It is easier to be a loving person than "be" the love that knows no person.

What then constitutes good citizenship? The ability to see man as Mind's awareness of its wholeness, and then to deal with one's brother from that withinness of consciousness. There can be no demonstration of true citizenship without the understanding of what constitutes the kingdom as individual man. To love one's neighbor as one's self is a divine idea. It has nothing to do with persons. This divine idea is the understanding that being is *one*. It is this understanding which elevates a community, a state, a nation to that state of consciousness where all interests are seen to be one interest as the one is *all*. If one would be a good citizen of the world, he must understand himself as Mind's reflection since as Mind's reflection every thought of man has the potency and intelligence of Mind. No man can serve his community or his nation until he lives his true selfhood as compound idea including all right ideas. Any time we see our brother as other than Mind's reflection of itself, which is one's own self in every quality of being, we have failed in true citizenship.

True Identification

Christian Science enables you to rise above all personal sense and actually identify all that confronts you as Mind, Mind's representation of itself. The ideas which you entertain of God are the substance and nature of your own true selfhood. Every idea is instantly serviceable to you, and can never fade out or deteriorate or disintegrate. These ideas are tangible and never in conflict of interest or activity. The allness of God predicates the oneness of all and every manifestation. This unity of being has no brotherhood. No individual or nation can consequently hold itself aloof from the affairs of other nations. The universe (man, I, consciousness) is one and is individual, undivided and indivisible. I am my brother's keeper since being is one universal I. This does not mean any assumption of what may seem to be his difficulties. We cannot be of any value in sharing what seems to be his ignorance. A teacher who does not work from the standpoint of Principle cannot help a student solve a problem in arithmetic. If we assumed the responsibility for the working out of his problems from within the seeming problem, we would fail in our love, which to be Love knows no problem.

"Jesus beheld in Science the perfect man . . . and this correct view healed the sick." Did he behold the perfect man with his eyes, or did he understand man as the pure manifestation of Mind, the Kingdom of Heaven, with no capacity to sin or suffer — therefore, undergoing no sin or suffering? Did not Jesus understand that man, wherever man seems to be, is present as all-inclusive consciousness or the I AM. Christ Jesus said, "And I, if I be lifted up from the earth, will draw all men unto me." The whole of that which constitutes being to me must rise as I rise, since it is I. Therefore, a Christian Scientist cannot be an isolationist. Man as the all-inclusive consciousness (the universe) includes the right idea of all that exists. Nor can a Christian Scientist really be an interventionist, since any attempt to intervene, or change the course of events for our brother man from within what is called the human existence, would be to entertain the illusion and attempt to improve it.

We cannot outline how Truth, unfolding as the consciousness of the individual, would appear to human sense; or what human steps may express the highest belief of human concept on the part of the Scientist who understands the divine reality. Nor can we outline how the dissolution of a false material concept, revealing man and the universe as it is, would appear to human sense, and the attempt to so outline would prevent scientific demonstration. Eternal Truth is changing the universe. (The one Ego or Principle) will overturn until (the one Ego or Principle) whose right it is will reign. This dissolution of material beliefs is described by Ezekiel: "I will overturn, overturn, overturn, it: and it shall be no more, until he come whose right it is; and I will give it him."

ABOUT THE AUTHOR: The papers of Martha Wilcox deal with the subjective consciousness and how it can be changed through an understanding of God. Mrs. Wilcox shows that change is inevitable when we treat the inner self through prayer as taught in Christian Science. The strong point of her writing is her emphasis on the need to so spiritualize the subjective self that it results in healing.

Martha Wilcox was a prominent teacher during the years when the Christian Science organization was at its peak of prosperity. She grew up on a farm in Kansas, under the influence of a religious family life. She studied privately for a Teacher's Certificate and became a teacher in the local schools. Before finding Christian Science, she was an active member of the Methodist Church. It was through a series of events, in which she sought medical aid for her ailing husband, that she was presented in 1902 with a copy of *Science and Health.* As she studied and pondered this book, she was healed of a physical problem of longstanding. While her husband was not interested in Christian Science, she definitely was.

Within the next six years, she had Primary class instruction, became an active member of a branch church in Kansas City, Missouri, and managed to devote much of her time to the healing work, in addition to caring for her family. In 1908 she received a call from The Mother Church in Boston asking her to serve Mrs. Eddy at her home in Chestnut Hill, Massachusetts.

In Mrs. Wilcox's first interview with Mrs. Eddy, it was

impressed upon her that everything in one's experience is subjective or mental. Mrs. Wilcox writes of this interview: "[Mrs. Eddy], no doubt, realized that at my stage of growth, I thought of creation — that is, all things — as separated into two groups, one group spiritual and the other group material. But during this lesson I caught my first glimpse of the fact that all right, useful things — which I had been calling 'the unrighteous mammon' — were mental and represented spiritual ideas. She showed me that unless I were faithful and orderly with the objects of sense that made up my present mode of consciousness, there would never be revealed to me the 'true riches,' or the progressively higher revealments of substance and things."

Mrs. Wilcox later wrote: "I well remember when for the first time I understood that everything of which I am conscious is thought, and never external to or separate from what I call my mind, and that which I call my mind is not always seeing things as they actually are."

In 1910, Mrs. Wilcox was recommended by Mrs. Eddy for Normal Class instruction, with Bicknell Young as teacher. This was the beginning of a long and successful career for Mrs. Wilcox as a practitioner and teacher. In 1911, she taught her first class. Until her passing in 1948, she was dedicated to serving the Christian Science movement, and became one of the most respected teachers in the Field. She was the author of many profound papers on Christian Science, mainly papers given each year to her association of students.

Mrs. Wilcox's two years with Mrs. Eddy equipped her to understand so well the subjective nature of all things. She explains how to shift the focal point of thought from the objective world of people, things, happenings, to the subjective world of intuitions, thoughts, ideas. Although she stresses the mental cause of disease and discord, she goes beyond an analysis of the human mind and explains how to relate to God subjectively through prayer; how to develop an understanding of Him that spiritualizes consciousness and heals, how to transcend the false material view of creation and find the spiritual view.

At the time that Mrs. Wilcox wrote these papers, the Church organization would not permit the publication or circulation of such papers. But Mrs. Wilcox did share them privately with students, and they were handed down over the years to the present time. In giving these papers to her students, it is possible that Mrs. Wilcox hoped they would someday go forth to bless a world so in need of their spiritual message.

For further information regarding Christian Science:
Write: The Bookmark
           Post Office Box 801143
           Santa Clarita, CA 91380
Call: 1-800-220-7767
Visit our website: www. thebookmark.com